Painting My Japan

Sheena Bradley

ISBN: 978-1-914130-29-8

This small volume is dedicated to all my family, with special mention and thanks to my Japanese family, Darragh, Yukie, Keigh, Yoko and Soichirou who hosted all my trips to Japan where these impressions were formed, and inspirations grown.

Calligraphy is by Keigh Tachibana Bradley

"Calligraphy is an art form that uses ink and a brush to express the very souls of words on paper."
— *Kaoru Akagawa*

日本

Contents

Wabi-sabi

Kintsugi art renews,
makes beautiful again
life's damaged things;
do not discard the broken chawan
dropped as the saké flowed.

Pink peonies glow
across mingled fragments,
radiate along the gilt,
grow strong with ikebana –
give pleasure in their difference.

Accept life's mutations.
Repair fractures with gold-laced resin,
love the glimmered glaze
as you treasured once the newly crafted bowl.
Contents fill it just the same.

Samurai's Seppuku

Rain obscures the mountains –
I sit under a chestnut tree
with white flowers falling;
leaf drips anoint my neck.
I welcome the closing dark.

It is easier to write the Jisei
than to face
the mystery of eternal darkness.
Schooled in calligraphy,
poetry and Zen –
bushido is my sacrament.

What if my stroke should miss
the major artery,
if guts alone should spill
and pain engulf me –
if death is not quick?

Aah, my tanto,
like my pen, draws true.
That gush of red
is proof, is life.

I bow my weakening neck
to the coming dark.

Way of the Warrior

Bushido code can be my only way.
Given a wooden sword when I was three,
I learned to serve. I live from day to day

long miles from those I love. My children play
without a father, my lonely wife must see
Bushido code can be the only way

for me to honour my beliefs and stay
within the brotherhood of Samurai.
We live to serve our shogun every day.

Loyalty to my Lord means I survey
his titled land and keep his family free.
Bushido code must be the only way.

It's always been my duty to obey,
behead his foe, disarm the peasantry;
to serve has been my life, my only way.

And now this battle is my last, since they
have killed my Lord Katsui, but spared me.
Bushido code is all that's left – this way
I serve him with my death. Yomi today.

Basho's Rebirth

Boughs of apricot and peach hang low with blossom
around my father's gate.
I am dragged from my mother's arms
and given a wooden sword
to be taught the art of fencing.

A blood moon skirts the crowns of walnut, birch and maple
near my uncle's home
and horses whinny in welcome as we arrive.
Archery and unarmed combat
replace my childhood games.

Autumn leaves swirl orange and ruby red
on the mock battlefield.
I recite the names of my ancestors,
the code used when rushing into battle
sword in hand.

Cedar and cypress slump down with snow
at the grave of Todo Yoshitada,
son of my lord,
my friend and brother.
I abandon the sword forever.

Cicadas, birds and frogs chirrup and croak
by my little hut, and the banana tree
gifted me by students.
I take its name: *Basho* –
more honourable than the sword.

Within The Wave

(After Hokusai - The Great Wave off Kanagawa. Woodblock Print, 1820-1831)

your eye

                            is drawn
                      to blue monsters
                  white claws curled
              to grasp what comes their way
              sucking guts   from small bodies

                tucked
              into curves
          of engulfing waves
          rushing West
          thirty   in skiffs
            dressed in blue
                out of Edo   passing Kanagawa
                  their lives   at the mercy
                      of the sea

you see

                      snow-clad Fuji
                          balanced
                            at the wave's heart
                          sacred
                        immutable

        not caring   that they will be swallowed whole.

Spear of Izanagi

Sibling Gods, we gaze with wonder
upon earth's blue-black velvet ocean –
now ours. The gate through which
we passed, closes behind us,
fades in a flurry of mist as we falter
on the swing and sway of slats beneath our feet.

I stand with you Izanami on this dark bridge
between earth and heaven, a red gold
halo of moonlight burnishes your hair,
the jewelled Spear of the Elders glitters
in my hand, entwined in the other,
your small fingers, warm and comforting.

Ahead lies the challenge of our future life,
to create order from chaos.
Taking strength from your smile, I grip
tight the naginata, reach across the rail
and swirl the blade in brine,
turn a whirlpool to turquoise.

I raise it high from the water,
call loud to Elder Gods for creation
of order, watch viscous drops
fall from the tip and spread to form
eight great islands, mountains,
rivers and trees.

A blazing orb crests the far horizon,
colours shine red, green and gold
in that sun-reflecting sea.
The bridge dissolves in mist as we descend together
and kneel to kiss the soil of our new home –
Our Land of the Rising Sun.

Izanami Gives Birth to Fire

I see you Izanagi, pushing
my first babies onto the ocean,
displeased they were
imperfect.

You blamed me
because I had spoken
before you
at the ceremony of union.

I smiled as we went through the wedding
again, teeth tight.
Your smile
also did not reach your eyes.

This time, you spoke first to ensure
that all our babies were divine,
Sea, Tree and *Mountain.*
Soon, you hankered after *Fire.*

Those early days are clear in my memory,
both Gods, both beautiful,
so honoured to be chosen
for this task, to bring order
to earth's chaos.

And how your muscles rippled
when the Elder Gods
gave you that jewelled spear.
My empty hands itched.

As *Fire* flickers
around my navel,
Izanagi, you are nowhere to be seen.

Sea, *Tree* and *Mountain*
are full in my vision,
but as flames consume me, I ask
where are my firstborn now?

Nijyuu Hibakusha

(Nagasaki - 9th August 1945)

Tsutomu stares at his steaming miso.
Hisako slams down her cooking pan,
and glowers.
You must be mad. You're sick.
You can't eat. You look terrible.
Your own mother doesn't know you –
calls you 'walking dead'.
A singed smell stirs the air
as Tsutomu shakes his patchy head.

When is this war going to end,
what sort of bomb have they made
that can do such damage?
No work today, Tsutomu. Stay home.
I'll go to the clinic, get salve for your burns.
He rises, lays a hand on her head – she feels
the heat of his burns, even through the bandages.
Tsutomu smiles and leaves for work.

At midday Hisako rocks the baby
beside the matchstick ruins of their house.
Tsutomu trudges home through bombed rubble.
You're alive! They cry in unison
and embrace, baby between them. Hisako sobs,
We were at the clinic for your ointment.
If you hadn't come home with your burns,
Katsutoshi and I would be dead. Tsutomu
smiles his meat-red smile.

Shinjuku Station

Chuo? Keio? Toei? Odawara?
Jingles and discordant announcements –
lost, hot tears fall.

Tanka for Tourists

with each hanami
tender sap green life bursts forth
national airwaves
herald our renewal
this season of rebirth

Unwanted Gift

Waterford crystal
shatters in an earthquake –
shards scatter rainbows.

Golden Week

Red lanterns glow,
Taiko drums reverberate
in a suburban street.

Frotteur

Tight-packed bodies meld
on the last night-train to Ichikawa
out of Tokyo Central.

Akihabara – Electric City

Handheld games,
rice cookers, Hello Kitty hairdryers:
gadgets for the scrapman.

Hiking from Kyoto

cherry blossom falls
carpets city streets
disarming commerce

        spring summons sap
        draws new life to lift and turn –
        cotyledons in sun

maple buds unfurl
caterpillars eat their fill –
a rooster crows

        camouflaged by green
        among fallen acorns –
        a praying mantis

in pelting rain
cosmos gleam at the verge –
we splash in the puddles

Harajuku

Ostentatious youths
give individual displays –
city peacocks.

Ikizukuri

The dish arrives on your table –
uniform translucent slivers
of sashimi

arranged like scales
beside that red snapper
you netted earlier –

pink-lustred, flapping,
fresh from the tank.
Now finely filleted,

skeleton exposed,
tail skewered
to upper body,

a perfect curve
of spine and ribs.
Mouth and gill gulp,

the one eye
appears to plead.
Its heart beats.

Nakasendo Way

Mitake-cho far behind, the Way ahead is clear;
an avenue of history, leaf-roofed, ascends to sky.
Once tightly packed to bear horses, palanquins
and thousands of reed shod feet,
these worn paving stones now curve steeply

into crevices of clustered geums
and forest primrose, glowing in the gloom.
Feet and ankles tilt with every step;
we climb toward light, breathing hard.
A pattering breaks through,

a thousand spectral hands soft-clapping.

In time, cooling splashes penetrate the canopy.
And still we march uphill, invigorated by rain,
accompanied by shushing footfalls,
echoes of a thousand Tokugawa shoguns,
daimyo, samurai and weary pilgrims.

Best view in Hakone
Fuji-San floats on mist:
invisible in the photograph.

Kiso Valley Walk

chipmunk on a picnic table
summer breeze rustles branches –
go-faster stripes

black clad monks arrive –
Magome villagers smile
fill wooden alms bowls

reflection on the lake
ripples as a grey heron dips –
catches breakfast

Peace Park

haunted by the shell
of the domed ruin
eased by the embrace
of Otagawa and Motogasu

lulled by the low toll
of the Peace Bell
people queue –
to ring for change

archways frame pain
pools of water
reflect that same sky
from which Little Boy fell

sun-scorched paving
stretches ahead
recalls images
from that August morning

of shadows
seared
onto fences
footpaths
doorsteps

Sadako Siseki

My father has seen
a thousand cranes
fly low over Miyajima,
their stuttering cacophony
a canticle to peace.

I am one of many
hibakusha here,
tossed through the air
near the Misasa Bridge
by the blast of Little Boy.

My family fled
as a dark cloud
eclipsed the sun.

Black rain fell.
But the true legacy came softly
from deep in my marrow.

I fight and I fold
a thousand cranes
so I can dance
a thousand years.

Sumo

Both
take
spider
stance, toes curled
to grasp solid ground;
balanced like boulders, muscles tense
as they rise on fixed flexed joints. One cannonballs forward–
girth wide, but feet like butterflies,
grabs the *mawashi,*
heaves – ousts his
foe from
the
ring.

Ten Past Six

They call us *rokuji jupun*
because our backs are bent
by life and weariness of time -
Nozomi, my given name,
no longer spoken.

I find my purpose
near Shukkei-en Gardens
before the city wakes,
I remove the stains of yesterday,
sweep it clean.

My spine will never straighten
but I am upright in my belief.
I do this for my country,
to keep it pristine
under the Rising Sun.

Walking Kyoto Streets

maiko girls in rain
red and yellow umbrellas
whiff of wet silk

green and red kimono
geisha on a Gion crossing –
traffic lights flash

Nishijin loom hums
weaves an obi – green on gold –
tourists at the door

Sleeping with Tigers

My hike-harried body drops
onto the dormitory futon
but brain cogs keep turning.
Snores from a sleeping bedfellow
join the rustle of my buckwheat pillow.

Light forges through rice-paper shoji
as the toilet flushes one more time.
Savour herbal hints of the tatami –
tally leaves of grass on that painted screen –
count those tigers into the stream.

Next morning, on the veranda of the hojo,
eyes open, legs flopped in lotus,
calm ... breathe ... omm ...
count those rocks. My focus lost –
fifteen baby tigers swim across.

Temple of the Peaceful Dragon

We waken early
for Ryoanji Temple Garden tour.
BBC World News reports
US cluster-bomb strike
on an Afghan village.

Paths shine white,
maples shed a ruby glow
in the low autumn sun;
cicadas hum in shrubbery
as babbling voices fade away.

An ornate white marble
memorial to seven Emperors
looms
a splash of chuckling ducks disturbs
the glassy blue of Kyoyochi pond.

We climb paved steps
to a temple courtyard,
Mondrian in grey and white
surrounded by Kandinsky bushes.
Birds ascend as we arrive.

Barefoot in the hojo
we glide onto cool fresh tatami,
hushed by symmetry;
incense filters the air,
a flameless dragon smiles.

In a dry landscape garden
fifteen rocks artfully placed
among raked white stones
reflect the discipline
imposed by centuries of monks.

A tinkle of temple bells
dispels the thrum of nearby traffic,
recalls cloisters,
cocoons us.

Winter in Chiba

winter willow
a droopy brown pom-pom
sways in the wind

      paper birch in snow
      bark peeling like wallpaper –
      we feel the cold

            sun pierces cloud
            illuminates a patch of field:
            momentary Spring

Painting My Japan

(After Van Gogh's copy of Utagawa Hiroshige's print
of Plum Park in Kameido, 'Flowering Plum Tree', 1887.)

People assemble at the fence,
drawn to the honeyed
efflorescence of ume,
as I am lured
in luminous February light
to their curling silk kimonos.

My hand melds with my brush,
takes me deeper into their floating world.
This Plum Tree
is in a Kameido Garden,
I am in Japan.

Imprisoned too long
by Agathorchas' optics
and clair-obscure,
now I see –
there is no darkness.

These blocks of colour, flat
and bold, enhance my vision.
The power of the diagonal
moves
the vanishing point,

the sun glows in its fullness,
these trees grow,
no longer shrink
to fit
man's constrained horizons.

My Mother's Tea Ceremony

No need for a painted silk kimono:
come as you are, in your flower-sprigged
wrap-around apron, her door is always open.

No need for a Sen-no-Rikyu chawan:
her fine porcelain was purchased
with Green Shield stamps.

No need for tetsubin or charcoal:
her kettle gleams on the stove,
boiling in seconds to warm the pot.

No need for green matcha powder:
finest leaves of black Assam nestle
in that gold lacquered caddy.

No need for wagashi to tempt your palate:
there's always her home-made sponge cake,
Ah, do have some. Yes, you will. Eat up.

And everyone must have a second cup.

Glossary of Japanese terms used.

Page 9 - Wabi Sabi : *a Japanese philosophy which calls for seeing beauty in the flawed or imperfect.*
Kintsugi means 'golden repair'. Breaks in ceramics are mended with gold resin. This repair method was also born from the Japanese feeling of mottainai, which expresses regret when something is wasted, as well as mushin, the acceptance of change. Kintsugi has become an art form.

Page 11 - Samurai's Seppuku : *Seppuku – ritual suicide as practised by the samurai.*
Jisei – death poem.
Tanto – short dagger.
Ikebana – the art of flower and plant arranging.
Bushido - the code of honour and morals developed by the Japanese samurai.

Page 13 - Basho's Rebirth : *'Basho' as a name, means 'banana plant'. Matsuo Basho trained as a samurai, like his father before him but when his friend, the son of his Lord died a natural death, he left to live the life of a Buddhist monk, write haiku and teach.*

Page 16 and 17 - Spear of Iznangi and Izanami Gives Birth : *In the Shinto Creation Myth, the gods Izanami and Izanagi create the eight great islands of Japan. They are the solidified drops from the tip of Izanagi's spear. Izanami dies giving birth to the Fire God.*

Page 19 - Nijyuu Hibakusha : *Hibakusha – the term used for someone who survived an atomic bomb in Japan.*
Nijyuu Hibakusha – someone who survived both atomic bombs.

49

Tsutomu Yamaguchi, aged 29 at the time, was one of about 165 people known to have returned home to Nagasaki after being bombed in Hiroshima, (6th August 1945), in time for the second atomic bomb. Tsutomu went on to father two more children and lived until he was 93. Eventually, he was the only Nijyuu Hibakusha left alive when the Government gave him an official award in 2009 (a year before his death).

Page 20 - Shinjuku Station : *Shinjuku Station in Tokyo is the world's busiest station, (used by a calculated 3.64 million people per day in 2007). 53 platforms from several lines can be accessed from its halls without surfacing above ground. There are more than 200 exits.*

Page 21 - Tanka for Tourists : *Hanami means 'flower viewing' and is the traditional custom of enjoying in particular the beauty of cherry blossoms. Families, friends and work colleagues gather in parks as the blossom begins to fall and hold rowdy parties which can last all night. There are regular National media broadcasts about where the blossom will be best witnessed falling - and some people, mainly tourists, travel from the South to the North of the country following the blossom and hanami parties.*

Page 24 - Golden Week : *a National Holiday week all over Japan at the end of April/ beginning of May. Originally it was to celebrate the birthday of the Showa Emperor. There are street parties everywhere and festivals in the major parks. In Tokyo, it frequently coincides with the best cherry blossom viewing.*

Page 30 - Ikuzukuri : *Ikizukuri are specialized restaurants where you are served the freshest fish available, alive. Often the customers catch their own fish from a tank in the atrium of the restaurant, before the meal.*

Page 31 - *Nakasendo Way* : *one of the two ancient routes between Tokyo and Kyoto, it passes through the mountains. The other is the Tokaido Road which passes along the East coast crossing several rivers. Only short sections of either remain in their original form.*

Page 36 - *Sadako Siseki* : *Sadako Saseki inspired millions with her fight to live and is commemorated in the Hiroshima Peace Park – The Children's Memorial - which is festooned with multicoloured paper cranes still made by school children all over the country and abroad. She died of radiation induced leukemia in October 1955, aged 12.*
Myth has it that cranes live for 1000 years and anyone who folds 1000 origami cranes can have a wish come true.

Page 37 - *Sumo* : *The name refers to the sport, a form of wrestling, or to the fighter. The 'ring' in sumo, called the dohyo, is a slightly raised circle of clay and sand mix on the ground. If a wrestler's foot crosses this line, a point goes to his opponent. Mawashi – The silk wrap worn by sumo wrestlers.*

Page 39 - *Ten Past Six* : *Translates to Rokuji jupun – the position of the hands on a clock reflect the bent over habitus of many of these elderly citizens who voluntarily clean the streets – unpaid.*

Page 40 - *Walking Kyoto Streets* : *Maiko – Trainee geisha. Gion – the geisha district in Kyoto.*
Nishijin – The traditional weaving district in Kyoto A few elderly weavers still exist, but the trade is dying out. The young are not taking up the family tradition and the intricate woven silks are very expensive – the trade almost totally dependent on tourist money.

Obi – the intricate and beautiful ornamental belt worn with the kimono.

Page 46 - Painting My Japan : *Ume – Plum blossom or the plum tree.*
Ukiyo-e – translates as 'The Floating World'. This was the name given to that part of Tokyo where these woodblock prints originated and became the name given to such prints.

Page 48 - My Mother's Tea Ceremony : *Sen-no-Rikyu – the traditional formal Japanese Tea Ceremony.*
Chawan – tea bowl.
Tetsubin – the container for boiling the water.
Matcha – powdered green tea.
Wagashi – Japanese sweets offered with tea.

ACKNOWLEDGEMENTS

I would like to express thanks to the editors of magazines in which many of these poems first appeared: mainly *Reach, Dawntreader and Sarasvati* – the Indigo Dreams publications, also to *Orbis* and the anthologies *For The Silent* and *Crossroads*.

Many thanks to Rory Waterman who tutored and mentored me most generously through this collection, which formed the basis of my Masters' Dissertation at NTU.

Thanks to my friends from the OU who read and re-read versions of these poems over many months (maybe it was years!) Patricia Osborne and Maureen Cullen, also, to my Masters' Mates, Josie Barrett and Jo Weston.

Later mentors who have helped immensely with editing the manuscript are Anna Saunders, Cathy Grindrod and *Impspired* Editor, Steve Cawte.

And of course, finally, thanks to my family for tolerating my obsession with poetry, which has taken over our dining room and bookshelves for the past few years.

About the Author

Sheena was born in a village near Draperstown in Northern Ireland and went to University in Dublin. She spent five great years in Liverpool and has now lived in Nottingham longer than anywhere else. She worked as a Radiologist in Grantham, Lincolnshire for 22 years, and since retirement has been writing, mostly poetry.

She loves words and images, but also mountains, bogs, beaches, birds, clouds, and all sorts of natural things.

Her eldest son lives in Japan with his family, and before travel restrictions entered our lives, she visited that country regularly and loved their rich history, culture, traditions and poetry which inspired her Dissertation for the MA in Creative Writing completed at NTU in 2018.

Many of these poems have been published in *Sarasvati*, *Dawntreader* and *Reach*, *(The Indigo Dreams Press)*. Her work has also appeared in *Orbis*, *The Beacon*, *As It Ought To Be*, *(AIOTB)*, *Poets' Choice*, *Dear Reader* and in *Impspired*.

OTHER TITLES FROM IMPSPIRED PUBLISHING

P.O.N.D – by John L Stanizzi

Stolen – by Candace Meredith

Masquerading as a Poet – by Charlotte Neal

Pondering the Shoreline of Existence – by Ann Christine Tabaka

Stepping Up – by DC Diamondopolous

Printed in Great Britain
by Amazon

62280736R00032